Spirit of Wild

KB Ballentine

"What did you want to be, when you thought you could / be anything?" asks poet KB Ballentine. The poems in this luminous collection emerge as beacons, offering guidance in brief moments bound in rich imagery. Some poems pose other questions: "How do I lose / part of myself / and stay whole?" Some offer gentle assurances: "To sing in the dark / is to know there is light." All attest to the resilience and persistence of the spirit, like "a rain of starlings in winter's longest night— . . . rising, always rising." Ballentine's unmistakable voice and skill with language shine throughout, balancing the natural world with the natural interiors of the human heart. What is the "spirit of wild" if not that pairing, that step into our truest selves as "the restless wind whispers courage." Find your courage in these poems.

Sandy Coomer, author of *The Broken Places*

As KB Ballentine delves without fear from windowed rooms into a wilderness of forest and ocean, it soon becomes clear that even the darkness in her collection *Spirit of Wild* is one that teems with life, wing, and song. In a place where "horses feed in the gloaming" and hope expresses itself with the music of chimes, time is marked only by the changing of seasons, the different names of the moon, and the pangs of the poet's grief. The spirits here are imbued with an astonishing empathy toward each other, a testament to the poet's own empathy as she opens herself to a wilderness which teaches her how to lose someone she loves. There are dissonances and dangers here, of course, but an untamed beauty transcends them. These well-crafted and well-arranged poems teach us to "cast off the rooms where we've boxed ourselves tight" and "step into the den of the forest's deep heart." Ballentine shows us that there is "a shelter for the sacred in each of us." *Spirit of Wild* is a balm, and I didn't know how much I needed it.

Chera Hammons, author of *Maps of Injury*

Spirit of Wild confirms that "each day waits with sudden mysteries, / offerings, / like dreams half-remembered / from the night." In lyrical, precise language that throbs and pulses with the rhythms of the natural world, Ballentine celebrates the spirit of all manner of life's organic wonders, from the fox and wren to the bee and seahorse, to lavender fog and "stones cloaked in mossy silence." Here, on a journey through changing seasons, under every phase of the moon, in real-time, dream-world, and memory, the poet illuminates – through motifs of light that linger, dissolve, glint, and leap – those wild spaces where we can safely mourn our absences or linger in the throes of desire. Emerging as we are from the pandemic, I can't think of a better time for this exuberant collection to come to light, nor a better time to heed Ballentine's call to "cast off the rooms where we've boxed ourselves tight / step into the den of the forest's deep heart."

   Hayley Mitchell Haugen, Sheila-Na-Gig Editions

Also by KB Ballentine

Edge of an Echo (2021), Iris Press
The Light Tears Loose (2019), Blue Light Press
Almost Everything, Almost Nothing (2017), Middle Creek Publishing
Perfume of Leaving (2016), Blue Light Press
What Comes of Waiting (2013), Blue Light Press
Fragments of Light (2009), Celtic Cat Publishing
Gathering Stones (2008), Celtic Cat Publishing

Anthologies containing Ballentine's work:

LOVE Anthology (2023)
Spirit : A White Stag Anthology (2023)
Appalachia (Un)Masked (2022)
Chattanooga Writers' Guild Vol. VI (2022)
Women Speak, **Volume 8** (2022)
Pandemic Evolution (2021)
Pandemic Puzzle Poems (2021)
The Strategic Poet (2021)
Voices in the Wind (2021)
Women Speak, **Volume 7** (2021)
20/20 Vision Focus on Scotland: A Poetic Response to Photography (2018)
Carrying the Branch: Poets in Search of Peace (2017)
In God's Hands (2017)
In Plein Air (2017)
River of Earth and Sky: Poems for the Twenty-First Century (2015)
The Southern Poetry Anthology, **Volume VI: Tennessee** (2013)
Southern Light: Twelve Contemporary Southern Poets (2011)
A Tapestry of Voices (2011)
The 2008 Poets' Guide to New Hampshire (2008)

Spirit of Wild

KB Ballentine

Blue Light Press 1st World Publishing

San Francisco | Fairfield | Delhi

Spirit of Wild
© 2022 by KB Ballentine

No part of this book may be reproduced by any means known at this time or derived henceforth without written permission of the publisher or author. The exception would be in the case of brief quotations embodied in the critical articles or reviews and pages where permission is specifically granted by the publisher or author.

Books may be purchased in quantity and/or special sales by contacting the publisher. All inquiries related to such matters should be addressed to:

1st World Library
PO Box 2211
Fairfield, IA 52556
www.1stworldpublishing.com
worldlibrary@lisco.com
(641) 209-5000

Blue Light Press
PO Box 150300
San Rafael, CA 94915
bluelightpress.com
BlueLightPress@aol.com

ISBN: 978-1-4218-3538-9
Library of Congress Cataloging-in-Publication Data

Cover Photo: KB Ballentine
Cover and Page Design: Jim Canestrari
Author Photo: Chris Wood
Interior Artwork: Alexandr Bakanov

Printed in the United States

Many of these poems have been previously published and are recorded on the Acknowledgments Page.

For the dreamers who stay awake.

Publication Acknowledgements

AFIELD: "Beauty Enough"
Black Moon Magazine: "Flesh Against Flesh" and "The Shape of Thorns"
Blue Mountain Review: "Almost Shining"
Blue Nib Poetry: "After We Collided"
Briar Cliff Review: "Shaped by Sadness"
Coffin Bell: "Revenant: Road of Song and Shadow"
Conch.es: "Hymn" and "Joy"
Crow & Cross Keys: "Midsummer Spell"
Door is a Jar: "A Winter Sleep"
Humana Obscura: "Write Your Name in Water"
Impressions: "If we just listen, we can hear ghosts"
Jimson Weed: "Luminescent"
Kakalak: "Refuge"
Kelp Journal: "A Song Already There"
Knoxville Writers' Guild: "Blown Like Seed" and "Valkyrie"
Linnet's Wings Christmas Canzonette: "Daughters of the Wind" and "Nesting Hymn for Winter"
Lothlorien Poetry Journal: "Interpreting Night," "Night Song," and "Wrapped in Snow-Light"
Louisiana Literature: "Redirection of Light"
LOVE Anthology: "A Tear in the Clouds"
Mock Turtle Zine: "Echoes, Frozen"
Montana Mouthful: "Second Skin"
Monterey Poetry Review: "Threading Space"
North Dakota Quarterly: "Crossing Dusk"
Orbis: "The Weight of Light"
Pandemic Evolution anthology: "The stars are always" and "Swept Away Like Stars"
Peacock Journal: "Unseen, Two Small Fawns"
Poetry Quarterly: "All Shall Be Well" and "Anthem of Spring"
Poppy Road Review: "Orion Holds Our Fate"
Quill and Parchment: "Disrupted Dreams," "Sea of Sighs," "Untethered," and "What I Owe the Fading Day"

Raconteur: "My next poem will be happy"
Rainbow Poems: "Song-Light"
Sheila-Na-Gig: "Green Persistence," "Hope, Thin as Silk," "Spirit of Wild," and "Wrapped in the Current"
Soul-Lit: "Trace the Light"
Spank the Carp: "Dr Tarr's Trout Farm" and "Moonwitching"
Sparked Lit: "The Promise of Stars" and "The Violet Hour"
The Strategic Poet: "One Thing I Desire"
Voices in the Wind anthology: "At the Joyce Kilmer National Forest"
Weekly Avocet: "Autumn, Taking Root," "Darkness Comes Alive," and "Memory of Moss"
Women Speak anthology, Vol 7: "Falling Between" and "Of Roots"
White Stag: Spirit anthology 2023: "Negative Space"

I am beyond blessed to have a network of friends and family who continually help and support me in my work, and I hope they know how much I love and admire them: Helga Kidder, Chris Wood, Diane Frank, Jim Canestrari, and Buddy and Susan Ballentine. Several workshop groups and my Open Mic members provide useful insight and comments, and I appreciate their help as well. To my faithful readers: thank you. Receiving your notes and emails keep me going when my mind is a blank page. You give me purpose and focus, and I appreciate you more than you'll ever know.

The breeze at dawn has secrets to tell you. Don't go back to sleep.

—Rumi

Contents

The Magnificent Cause of Being   1
My next poem will be happy   2

I

Luminescent   5
Threading Space   6
The Violet Hour   7
A Tear in the Clouds   8
The stars are always   9
Dissolving   10
Write Your Name in Water   11
Unseen, Two Small Fawns   12
Swept Away Like Stars   13
Blown Like Seed   14
Wrapped in the Current   15
Sea of Sighs   16
Redirection of Light   17
Negative Space   18
One Thing I Desire   19
Shaped by Sadness   20
Second Skin   21
Autumn, Taking Root   22
Back to Wonder   23
Falling Between   24

II.

Spirit of Wild	27
Memory of Moss	28
If we just listen, we can hear ghosts	29
Revenant: Road of Song and Shadow	30
Crossing Dusk	31
Wrapped in Snow-Light	32
Echoes, Frozen	33
Nesting Hymn for Winter	34
A Winter Sleep	35
December Meditation	36
Darkness Comes Alive	37
Drink the Moment	38
Disrupted Dreams,	39
Trace the Light	40
Anthem of Spring	41
Joy	42
Almost Shining	43
Untethered	44
Song-Light	45
Silver on the Pointed Twigs	46

III.

Green Persistence	49
After We Collided	50
The Weight of Light	51
Moon Haze	52
Aurora Wakes	53
Handful of Dust	54
Hope, Thin as Silk	55
Refuge	56
Of Roots	57
Flesh Against Flesh	58
At the Joyce Kilmer National Forest	59
The Smell of Summer Grass	60
The Shape of Thorns	61
Midsummer Spell	62
Orion Holds Our Fate	63
What I Owe the Fading Day	64
Night Song	65
As Light Dissolves	66
The Surface of Water	67
Winter, Taking Root	68
Interpreting the Night	69

IV.

Dr Tarr's Trout Farm	73
The Song Gathers	74
Daughters of the Wind	75
Beauty Enough	76
Valkyrie	77
Moonwitching	78
Evensong	79
The Promise of Stars	80
All Shall Be Well	81
Hymn	82
A Song Already There	83

The Magnificent Cause of Being

Taking advantage of a sun-fogged sky,
    I weed through fern and vinka, roots refusing
  the light. Hints of rain in air that wraps my skin.
Yellow jackets, home harnessed under hostas,
    scorch my palm   with sting   after sting,
      thrust chills   into my belly and   spine
until I lean against the oak,   yard tilting
     just a little   to the left.   I tug off gloves,
   watch welts erase   the shape   of my hand.
Thunder cracks: a drop then   two and   more
   until the sky crashes   and asphalt hisses and   steams.

Inside I pull vinegar, honey, baking soda —
every ingredient in plastic, glass, or cardboard
that might ease the pain, rain sliding, smudging the day.
In the dimness, orchids and violets pulse.
Potted and screened, never knowing weeds,
growing without need of anything
but water: here are the tame, the beautiful.
Never a kiss from a butterfly, a bee.
Sweetness shared only in still rooms,
windows overlooking the wild.

My next poem will be happy

because your eyes are the sea –
spray and foam of excitement,
bright and flickering with joy

because your hands know
how to soothe and caress,
how to hold a hammer or a broom

because your laugh fills
the room and you chuckle
over the comics and the ads

because you spot the red-herring
I never notice, and you show me,
again, how to tie the knots

because you kiss me a dozen
ways: daisies on my pillow,
love notes by the coffee cup,
splitting the last piece of chocolate

because you share your thoughts
as we re-make the bed,
as you cook and I clean dishes –

my next poem will be happy
because you
            are

I.

This is how it begins…

Luminescent

For my part I know nothing with any certainty, but the sight of the stars makes me dream. —Vincent Van Gogh

Telescoping through space and time,
stars fling energy across the galaxy.
   They escape the darkness and dust,
vibrate into dreams that glimmer
   waiting for wishes.

We hang our hopes on comets
   that scatter stone and flame
erasing shadows from the heavens.
Some people say our spirits blaze trails
   and flare the sky when we're gone –
all our stardust illuminating
   the hearts of those left behind.

Sometimes I think we are the darkness –
veils twined around those pulsing lights
   masking the earth, the moon,
clusters of dreams,
   sparks tucked into the belly of our sleep.

Threading Space

Crossing dusk is the first step:
right into the night where no stars are,
no moon to sigh your name.
Once through, there are no shadows –
only sounds of those singing around you.
Some songs have the low, flat notes of the blues
and others the anger of electric guitars
plucking each string over and over
until you want to screech a counterpoint.
But, if you keep going, over at the edges
where honeysuckle infuses the air,
you'll hear a simple chord,
then voices lifting in unison,
drawn to this melody.

A crescendo of arpeggios resonates
then a clear soprano fills the darkness.
A chorus hums, echoes throughout
this dim space and then –
just where the horizon unravels –
                              the severing of night.

The Violet Hour

Silver rain stitches the distance,
lavender fog glacier-moving across the morning,
trees and shrubs vague, ghost-like.
Though redbuds and cherry blossoms color
the woods, I can't see it. The last of winter's
logs warm the hearth. I hesitate, torn
between staying in or stirring outside,
smidgens of mist breathing my skin.

Beyond the hazel wood, fairy pools call,
small waterfalls a beacon for the lost, the lonely.
I am mesmerized by the thought of diving under,
bubbles of air enclosing, eclipsing my view –
like looking out this window,
                              waiting.

A Tear in the Clouds

Velvet leaves of lambs' ears
sprout along the woodline,
and mist kisses
the canopy of trees.
A melody of robins,
cardinals rings from somewhere
in the white veil.
The Lady of Shalott
was *half-sick of shadows*,
but the shadow of your soul
breathes in me.
How do I lose
part of myself
and stay whole?
Each day a lesson
in fatigue, no matter
if the day is warm
or the sky dark
or, like today,
hazed in its own charm
of here-not-here –
my favorite.
I can almost touch you
on days like this.
Memory or real, does it matter
when a goldfinch
at the feeder is the last
bright spot
before dusk descends?

Today in my heart / a vague trembling of stars.
—Federico Garcia Lorca

The stars are always

already before me. The light of dying
suns has been reaching me forever.
Difficult to brood when a certain charm
wraps these flecks of light
that etch and spangle the night.

Even a long and weary day can't chase
away hope when dusk descends,
and we're left sighing in the light
of a million million miles of dreams
dusting the galaxy, moon hovering
like an anxious mother.

Larks and katydids chorus the wind as it curves
this blue-green marble suspended
in emptiness. Illuminated by our own failing
sun, reflecting the last of its passion,
we, too, tremble at the darkness waiting –
                                        waiting.

Dissolving

> *You know how it feels, / wanting to walk into / the rain and disappear.* —Mary Oliver

Light lingers though clouds streak the west,
crowd closer while I watch rain sheeting before it arrives.
A thorn pierces my chest,
wind wandering the leaves
as a torrent of drops smacks the canopy,
lightning cracking the sky.
Even the birdsong has stopped under this barrage,
and nothing can divert the pain –
your absence like the fog seeping in,
                                  surrounding me.

I should go inside, flip on the lights, the television,
anything to bring the world back to life.
Why bother?
There's no warmth in LEDs and no reality
without a script. No, the emptiness,
the spinning mist are truth, are fact for now.
I need only abandon the porch and step
into that visible darkness.
                              Disappear.

Write Your Name in Water

It was the last visit – now our old excuses
will drift and shrivel like layers of snow.
How could we know?
Windsweep and wild waves echo
my thoughts. I almost hear
your voice, almost discover
where you are then I wake
to gray and dark.

Rain-slicked asphalt, trees half-shelter,
half-shower: silent sirens as we make our way
to the graveyard. Magpie crouching
on a limb – *one for sorrow*.
I need you to know you were on my mind,
I need you to know.
I need you.
Regret, like vinegar, bites my soul.

When these clouds creep through,
will I notice the blue?
And you? Can you still taste the rain
on my skin, ocean blurring its salt with mine?
Below the tide line, scattered shells and stones,
sandpipers calling,
                searching.

Unseen, Two Small Fawns

Redbuds vein the woods, purple
pulsing through leaping green.

Spring erupts in laughing daffodils,
cherry blossoms clustered in clouds,
gasping, gazing into the wind.

Moss retreats to the wood line,
as daylight lingers, forsythia bursting.

At the coast, wind lathers waves,
gulls shrieking in the shallows.

Afternoon sun tags shadows,
warms sand and rock, pools stranded by the tide.
Inking the sky, pelicans trail the horizon,

and, in hedgerows, wrens scuffle
with song, nuthatch descending the oak,
drawing down the night.

Swept Away Like Stars

Kuiper Belt: A6

Just past the heart, the mind
   is memory. Smudged
with fuzzy images of park picnics,
     combing grandpa's hair,
and blankets tucked tight at night –
   later bits brittle and scarred:
moons of memory where even ice dazzles
     and new horizons eclipse comets
that howl across the sky.
   A ring of longing walks with her
tugging some toward, thrusting others away –
     her own flaming sun burning off-course,
   burying what's left in ash.

Blown Like Seed

> *Now that the bones are gone, who lives in the final dust?*
> —Pablo Neruda

Look for me under your boot soles says Whitman;
        but my bones will long be dust –
blown and settled, settled and blown
                before the wren sings her brood to dream.
And if my dust slips through butternut forests
          on the paw pad of a lynx, what atoms remain
                will leap in joy as rain dribbles bits and parts
            into crevices of stone to stay,
to sprout meadowsweet or fern –
            or even bleed into ground water that seeps into the sea.
Ahh – to be part of a heaving mass of peak and trough,
                particles of salt kissing an echo of my lips.

Wrapped in the Current

I have been dreaming seals
   in an ice-edged dawn,
the blue of a nightingale's flight
   scattering into pixie dust.
Wavelets lapping a shingled shore
   urge me toward the sea,
sable eyes peeking above the water's rim.
   What do they see from the other side,
heads nipping in silence
   through half-water, half-sky?

The ocean embraces them, bodies spiraling,
   gliding, curling in a kind of grace.
Whatever follows, whatever their fears
   is not here, in this moment, in this place.
Their whiskers, my hair salt-soaked,
   frost riming my clothes, I breathe the deep.
Even in sleep I am moon-witched
   by the thrusting, tugging tides:
the rumble of the foaming, spraying surf,
   curving under and above, giving birth
to whirlpools and rhythms of bliss
   where seals frolic in tempests
and sing in my dreams.

Sea of Sighs

Mead Moon trips, spilling
the last of her honeyed light
over fields of fruiting hawthorn.
Horses feed in the gloaming,
the shortest night only days away,
snorts and nickers swelling
the wren's lingering song.
Crackle static of heat-lightning
over waves. Relentless
against the rocks, they throb
and pulse far below,
where cliff embraces sand,
pebbles and shells tossed with the spray.
Even an acorn grips the shore,
tracing the hope of a mighty oak
before the turning of the tide.

Redirection of Light

Past meadow and ridge, the ocean breathes.
   Shadows shaped like seahorses wriggle and squirm,
and the Mead Moon drizzles honey-light
     over rosebuds curled tight.
Petals eager to flare,
   to smoke the air as hazy days slide
into these short, bright nights
     when thistle and heather purple the hills.
When the cuckoo croons his melancholy tune
   to the rabbit in her burrow while the barn owl waits.
Green sings in summer dusk,
     stones cloaked in mossy silence
               as we lean toward the darkening.

Negative Space

> *Whatever the color and condition of things, open your eyes.*
> —Ghalib

Even if it's gray, open your arms wide.
And when the rain falls, lift your head,
open your mouth – it's not all about the eyes.
It's taste and touch, sound and smell.
Or the absence of.
The blank place that used to be *us* –
a hole that floods my whole being.
There's no color there,
and with my eyes wide open, I see it all: too clearly –
there. Just where raindrops shimmer
on the overgrown grass, between leaves of witch hazel
where silver glints and spools.
The place where you used to be.

One Thing I Desire

Like leaves shredded from a winter-stormed tree,
somewhere else teases, just beyond what I can see.
Branches tangle with vines, clack in icy cocoons,
but a bit of blue beckons.
                      Too much time alone
finds me addicted to self, even if, like Frodo of the Shire,
I began this journey in good faith, a service to others.

Now the novelty, the adventure of all I can do
from one house, one room has flattened my horizon
and forged a ring of *one* around all I do, all I say
to the virtual world.
                    I am a collection of atoms colliding,
hurling bits and bytes of electrons across the atmosphere
to Kansas, Florida, Ireland
to gather in separate spaces on one screen –
time meaningless.
                Sun and moon nudged ever farther
until fog and ice demand our witness.
Lights out. Networks down.
            We wander the darkness.
Each clover leaf just fragile enough to tear
but rooted together gentling the fall.

I want to see, to know you. I want to touch you again.

Shaped by Sadness

    Contralto breeze ricochets the cliffs,
waves thudding a crescendo.
    Siren moon singing over the sea, I wait
for you to enter my dreams.

    My toes dig into sand and silt that tug,
draw me to your arms, to the deep
    where I can sink, settle into cords of seagrass
and breathe – breathe the sting of salt,

    a chorus of bubbles soaring – urging me to stir,
to (re)emerge by way of rock, by stone,
    clinging to each rough edge until a verse
of sky or tree snags me back

    to the rhythm of stars swallowed by darkness –
moon a pearl, luster and song dissolving
                               like seaspray.

Second Skin

I could be a mermaid singing in the surf –
    bright Dyan moon glittering
  over wavelets like a honeycomb.
The drumming, thudding pound
    around cliffs and crags, ragged gasps
  of seaspray like diamonds,
like stars fragmenting,
    dropping back to earth.

  Nothing on land lures me –
not hawthorns fermenting the fields,
    not hares hushed under apple trees,
  not even laughter and lights from houses and pubs.
I might be swayed by a willow spilling branches into a river
    or by cows shape-shifting into manatees,

  but, no – I'd rather leap with dolphins,
mimic seahorses using only my fin to ripple
    through deeper tides while my hair weaves
  wild with salt and seaweed past the thermocline.
Whale fall and ship wrecks,
    starfish and kelp, a whirlpool of worlds
  under a membrane of brine –
a castle, a kingdom, my only home.

    With the sea over my shoulder,
  the moon-stream will sink
over murmuring seals, waves winding
    coastlines, washing and weathering
  each shingled shore. Every sand grain
and pebble rolled to its core.

    Over reefs, past jellyfish,
  salt-stung, flirting with storms
and white-caps crashing, racing with salmon
    past gardens of anemones – the sea summons
  me till I sing with the surf
in a necklace of foam,
    uncharted on maps, the ocean
  wide and open – all of it mine.

Autumn, Taking Root

A fugitive blue sneaks through
   the robe of dusk, mauve and purple
trembling in mist. Magnolias spy
   with cardinal eyes, and I eavesdrop
as stars hum a sickle moon into the sky.
   Abelia perfumes the air
and shadows calico the yard:
   Wait! Wait!
The edge of summer, the lip of change
   kisses this hour,
and we're all bewitched by whispering
   stones and starshine.

Back to Wonder

What did you want to be, when you thought you could
   be anything? When butterflies could surge
into shooting stars, when the sun sprouted
   like beans in your heart? When blue meant wonder
and mint remained bliss – a bluebird's egg
   could hold Niagara's kiss? Storybook charms sang
like polished plums, when thundering clouds
   spun into silver and pixie dust?

What did you want to be before evening-lilac turned
   semi-sweet and sparkling sage faded to haze?
When riverbed smoke blustered into city storms,
   and gray flannel refused to warm anymore?
When a whimsy of whiskers bit like sharkskin and bone,
   and sleeping giants awakened in a whirlwind of ash?

Let honey-light breathe like a fawn in the field,
   and the winter-bright night shelter like a shifting shield.
Think of spring thaw when the world's hidden in ice,
   when the cost of *anything* wasn't surrender or sacrifice.

Falling Between

This is how it begins:

    leaves brushed with yellow in the trees,
  a hawk's shadow masking parched roses,
whispers of rain ghosting the ridge.

    Figs bruise the yard –
sticky patches abandoned by all but bees and ants.

Wrapped in these last warm days,
    we walk through wood-light,
  the rumor of autumn closing in,
mountain laurel and ferns curling in blistered clusters.

    Fewer bird calls in the sweetgum, the cedar,
  silence surging like a drowning tide
though two deer lift their heads through leaf-gold.

    We wind our way past tulip trees, purple hearts
  tucked deep against the coming chill,
lose the light as gray sweeps overhead,
    mist pearling into firmer drops.

  One last breath before heading inside,
the taste of leaving on our tongues.

II.

bits of glitter / grabbing the light

Spirit of Wild

To sing in the dark
   is to know there is light

   like a fox shrugging the flame in its fur
the rush of the creek after a summer storm

the whisper of wings as an owl haunts by
   a nest of bones where daffodils peek

   sap surging upwards to green and then leaf
branches that creak through the wind's endless sigh

though shadows may shift and re-shape their forms
   let the wedge of the moon act as a lure

   cast off the rooms where we've boxed ourselves tight
step into the den of the forest's deep heart

Memory of Moss

Cushion and Broom: you are what we see,
   no explanation needed for your name, your charm;
Fountain moss: oh lover of streams and ponds but reluctant
   to trust the flow, clutching root and rock;
Carpet: like so many dense mats draped across the woody
   floor, plucked to stuff comforters, folk tales certain you
   give the gift of sleep;
Apple: with your russet shoots, you blossom bony hillsides;
Fringe: with a fondness for rocks and stone walls, you grip
   the edges of roofs and streams, always at the margins –
   the outlier;
Granite moss: softening colder climes, green against the
   slate, the ever-falling leaves;
Feather: with your quills; Hair-cap flowering green
   fireworks;
Bog moss: with sprays like threads, a single bud blushing
   the field;
Star: as numerous as your namesake, as steady and
   stalwart, ready to handle anything, grow anywhere;
Elfin-gold and Luminous, you gloss cave walls,
   gleam in fissures and hollows, cradled in roots, light
   hidden
                                      but burning still.

If we just listen, we can hear ghosts

in the fog as it ribbons the fields waiting for dawn,
in rain as it splashes oak leaves,
even in shadows that hide the detritus of the day:
tote bag, mail, crumpled clothes.

These ghosts are the friendly ones,
the ones who grin when we flinch
at them peeking from the gloom.
The others (the ones inside our minds) –
those are the ones to dread.

They emerge at odd times and places,
stamp a memory across the *Now*
and expect a seat at Joyce's table
(whether we want them there or not).
What if we don't want to listen?

What if we can't hear anything else?

Revenant: Road of Song and Shadow

Meet me at the lamppost   at the end of your drive
when orange slides into purple,   slips into black,
   and we   tiptoe
past the trees until we're free, and I see you   for the first
   time –
like the last time,   only older. Not wiser but   sadder.
Unsure.
Laughter in your eyes   escapes your lips,
   fingers teasing
this skin,   my skin. And we share   memories
   of our youth –
the   *Remember when –*   and   *Oh yes, that was fun –*
or heartbreak.
Either way,   with you it was   right.
Real.
Shadows thick   with longing swallow our   desire.
   We struggle
past the curve, up the river   of road, hardness   hitting our
heels,   sinking
into our bones, our faces gray and shifting.   Back
   to where the lamppost sputters –
this one   last time.

Crossing Dusk

The dead don't leave us –
   hopes calloused and aching,
      mournful hymns crawling through our veins
   hoarding each memory
that burdens and bitters our days.

The dead don't leave us
   pierced with pain, clinging
      to empty spaces where we seek
   that fleeting warmth, their scent,
in the nest of shared history.

The dead won't leave us
   hiding in what's left of our mess
      as we sob, sowing sorrow
   at others' feet, make them wrestle
with our weeds and thorns.

The dead can't leave us –
   our foolish longings and worn out grief.
      They gaze at us from wherever they are,
   scaling the stars, witness to a light
they wait for us to see –

      No – we leave the dead –
   the timbre of their voices fading,
faces blurring, orphans of the heart
   who scatter sunlight
      as it burns low then disappears.

Wrapped in Snow-Light

In the Old Place
   muskox drift and foxes trot
through snow, flakes gusting
   like a blizzard of dogwood blossoms
through air stripped of moisture,
   parched and stinging like thorns.
Polar bears and seals leap
   across floes, gliding
under cracks, through leads
   until they loll, exhausted, together
in an archipelago of blue ice,
   jagged edges. Ink-dark sea,
blinding sky – absorbed in arctic dreams.

Echoes, Frozen

The language of winter speaks –
   hums through the air on crystals of ice
tinkling like chimes. They linger
   on brambles, bits of glitter
grabbing the light, flecks sparkling
   as wind sculpts then erases the horizon.
Evergreens whisper, powder shushing all
   but the groan of bare limbs tangling
in the wind. Branches cradle each letter,
   each word frozen in my throat, on the page –
rime of frost shimmering on news,
   on promises you will not hear.
I've strung them from sighs and tears,
   from a season of silence
that has yet to let grief sound like glasses clinking,
   shining in the frozen sun waiting for the thaw.
Breath a shapeless vapor. Mid-winter bitter
   and hungry – spring a long way off.

Nesting Hymn for Winter

My animal spirit celebrates the creatures
who hibernate these long and frosty nights.
To rest snug in a burrow, a den,
to let the ice blow in – all unaware.
No pricking holly or bitter wind
to sting my skin. No rifling
through snow for a snippet or bite.
No, my saving grace would be to hide away,
allow the cold moon's crescent
to cradle my dreams of strawberry moons,
a stray leaf blowing through shadowy gloom
sounding hopeful to slumbering ears,
like warm summer rain.

A Winter Sleep

A snowy owl grips my dreams,
strokes the shadows with silent wings.
The wind shares secrets with spits of ice,
tangling trees and curving them low.
A pocket of darkness etches the light
where Saturn and river stones sing in the night.

Buckwheat and honeycomb perfume the air –
an unfound door waiting sheltered and bare
where foxes dance and purple grapes entice.
Gusty and golden, hope soughs past the doe
wheeling through maple leaves swirling the wood –
hazy impressions of summer's childhood.

Restless regrets are hobbled by embers of stars
scoffing at fireflies caught in their jars.
The heart of the fig sobs like birds in disguise,
and haystacks are bundled and speckled with snow
while moonlight shards clouds in the silver-fox skies
weaving thunder and roses out of my sighs.

And the eye-bright owl bobs as he clutches and stings,
tugging me further inside of my dreams.

December Meditation

When winter stalks into view

let the fringe of day stir,
finches and bluebirds mimicking the sun

let buds shaped like nails
pierce magnolias' waxy leaves then blossom

let the lazy buzz of a wasp
remind you that summer soon greens

let dawn's chill and later flame
fill you with tomorrow's promise

Darkness Comes Alive

A rain of starlings in winter's longest night –
   a negative of white and black,
  breathing shadows inked by shadows.
     Faint flecks echo, reflect
     obsidian sky glossed with stars.

     Skimming sable woods, each sooty wing
     flicks, whisks the snow,
  ebony clouds changing shapes, whispering –
  whether it be hard as onyx or soft as pitch –
but rising, always rising, again.

Drink the Moment

A confession of snow sheets the roads,
washes the sky white, and we wait,
warmth measured in wool socks, mittens.
Snow tastes like winter she says to her big sister,
tongue stuck out to savor fat, wet flecks,
cheeks pinking with the cold.

The applause of crows startles us
as they shift from ditch to hickory,
branches cradling falling flakes.
Kids smudge the hill in streaks of color,
laughter frosting the air, ice crystals rising
around us even as evergreens droop in early twilight.

I have belonged to you since the beginning of time. —Mina Loy

Disrupted Dreams,

and moonlight shards the back yard,
dances between limbs just fledging.
You are the bright coin at the bottom of the well,
the wish that came true –
cello notes that linger after the leaping flute fades,
your voice a song in my veins.
It is you who fills me with courage,
the steady pulse when I'm afraid.
You are double-mellow on my tongue,
just breathing you is lightning on a nail.
Go to your happy place, she said,
and once again I stared into your eyes,
a wayward wind tickling the chimes,
returning home – always to you.

Trace the Light

Wild roses in late February,
saucer magnolias purpling the yard,
and Tir na nÓg emerges with tonight's sunset.
How did I get so lucky?
A sparrow sweeps past, joins the treetop chorus.

Though you are no longer here, I think of you –
how you would have made this moment linger.
Grass cooling in the coming dusk,
your arms around me, lips whispering my neck.

For a moment, I do remember Paradise.

Anthem of Spring

> *If you suddenly and unexpectedly feel joy, don't hesitate.*
> —Mary Oliver

Stars breathing in the night sigh
   as dawn erases darkness, erases gray,
day sliding across the horizon.
   Weary of winter, bees lisp, stumble
over new blooms. The thinnest edge
   of rain silvers the grass, mist curling
the top of the ridge. A moment of joy,
   wholeness soaring in your heart.
Not enough to watch butterflies dance
   over zinnias, but you must try
to stroke their gossamer brightness,
   promise to keep them safe.
In the still-damp yard, a symphony
   of color sings with the bees.

Joy

Mud crusts her paws, silky underbelly
   matted with knots, tangles of gold caked brown.
She whines, nudges my face as I bend to brush
   away the labor of her day. She squirms
under my touch and gnaws a twig, pieces
   of bark stuck to her muzzle. Day uncluttered,
unconcerned, she lopes through leaves,
   dodges joggers, licks the kids' faces.
She sees a squirrel and gives chase,
   barks a warning and a greeting.
Her head lolls, tongue flapping, as I scratch her sides.
   Her panting eases, and she snuffles
before her eyes close, tail twitching in ecstasy.
   Would that I could breathe so free –
to greet strangers as friends, find happiness
                         in a broken stick.

Almost Shining

Spring still brittle,
   chill grips the early morning,

flings the bleak season back at us
   while we hide behind daffodil smiles,

new-green leaves shivering the trees.
   Cotton-clouds scatter wishes

across the blue, above furrows fractured
   with cosmos dreaming, still

dreaming, in the half-light.

Untethered

The Plough Moon rides faultlines
of the wind, licks the sea with light
as Pisces scales the sky though frost tickles
the cedars. Milky vapor hazes the heath.
A fox, nose lifted, disappears
into the hazelwood, forked arrow
of an adder tonguing the mist.

Crickets grieve under starlight,
and the bay echoes the graves –
gray and hushed, shadowed. Riptide tugs,
sand sloughing the shingle,
clusters of eelgrass swaying, flowing
like a mermaid's hair drifting,
washing away with the phantom of dawn.

Song-Light

    after Mary Oliver

I listen for *the almost unhearable sound*
of the roses singing and sense the almost
unfeelable silk of the leaves greening.
Apple blossoms frisk as light shifts,
brightens – lingers.
Blank, gray days forgotten
except for the slight bite of morning's breeze,
hope tinkling in the chimes.

My neighbor waves, dazed
after another night at his mother's bed,
visible darkness drifting behind his eyes.
The restless wind whispers *courage*.

Up and down the street, dogs greet joggers
in a raucous crescendo that stutters to a stop.
Robins dimple the yard for worms, and the wren
– the plain brown wren – pipes and trills
until my very skin vibrates, sighs with the sun.
Last season crumbles, swept away by the *almost*
                            all around me.

Silver on the Pointed Twigs

Wisteria drips in lavender mist
   no bees yet in the delicate cups,
perfume infusing April's dawn.
   Leaves, forsythia, everything weeping
as titmouse and cardinal chant in the gloom.
   Where are the mourning doves?
This weather belongs to them.
   Dogwood blossoms dance, hum
in the drizzle. I hear you
   whistling, answering the birds,
but I can't see you.
   Fog thickens, pales into canvas
where crows silhouette the pines,
   chuckle and grunt from branches
before stretching their wings,
   vanishing into the unknown –
somewhere – with you.

III.

our honeycombed hearts / weave fire

Green Persistence

Light leaps from the Pink Moon
this early April morning.

You in my mind again.

Spring a puzzle in blossom and chaos –
brief chill, haunting warmth.

Cherry, redbud, dogwood feather the woods,
yards still gripped by shadows.

Filaments of green nudge the soil,
lift leafing heads to the sun.

Brown thrashers, orioles chitter
near thickets littered with nest-building,
a squirrel basking on the porch railing.

Even the air breathes beginnings –
but I'm stuck, struck still
as the past collapses
                    inside me.

The moon blinks and fades,
a blank canvas bluing the day.

After We Collided

        after Joy Harjo

I was a star falling from the night sky,
a cloud weeping on the horizon,
a feather stretching wide the wing,
a salmon scaling from ocean to river,
a seed unfolding in the soil,
a sigh in the hollow of your neck
and *I needed you to catch me.*

The Weight of Light

Quarried light of stardust –
    here we are.
We wait for the memory of aeons to rush back,
but we have forgotten,
our minds tangled in darkness,
in mystery.

Salt-scent fins of ocean –
    we return.
The shape of water on our tongues,
we are the voice of every wave
translating, rasping the shore.
Liquid silk fluent in rock, shingle, sand.

In the belly of the earth,
    our honeycombed hearts
weave fire through veins, coal and diamond
stitching our roots, so we breathe in heat, breathe out
the ash scorching our bones
now crucibled, pure.

Leaf-storms laugh, blossom-rain spiraling
    dusk into dawn:
where we dwelled with ache and worry, with indecision,
a silhouette of song pierces the thickets,
chimes swallowing wind –
harmony, lightning blazing into
                    the stuff of stars.

Moon Haze

River side spirits settle with fog,
 pearl the air with gossamer veils.
  Late night, early mornings are best to surprise
a glimpse, water chafing the banks,
 drowning their sighs, their steps.
  The darkness embraces their form.

A bit of mist detaches from the rest,
 a patch shifting its own way –
  maybe toward you, stroking your face
before you open your eyes to the stars
 and night's clearing, a small tendril
  flickering goodbye.

Aurora Wakes

A splinter in eternity, a thistle shedding thorns –
this gloaming haunts her with gray. Then the wind speaks,
mock-orange suffusing the language of day.
She casts her pearls over the mountain,
valley limned with light, shadows now thin as a knife:
the price for a helix of lavender, peach, and rose.
The vibration of her song arches across the fields,
swallows and spring peepers forget shyness,
peer into eyes wiser than blue laced with clouds
racing from the west to greet her.
                              Time torn and healing.

Handful of Dust

> title from TS Eliot's *The Wasteland*

Orchid arches, purples room's corner,
stretching for light as shadows lengthen.

No one sees what is in between
the trees that stand watch over the unknown,

oak and poplar nodding acquaintance
as dusk settles the horizon.

Made of starflakes, I am destined for the sky
though this dark heart holds me down.

Anvil or anchor?
I must decide which weight –

the heaviness of love
or the lightness of mercy.

Hope, Thin as Silk

Quicksilver moon unsettles
the velvet canvas of my sleep –
palpable dreams shifting
    into the almost-invisible.
I slip to the porch, seams of sea-light
stretching past the dunes, inviting me,
   wind singing in my ears.
No Selkie, but I long to cross to water's edge,
to stride into the surf until it slides under,
cradles me – forgives me of everything.

If I keep going, will I find you at the horizon?
Or are you closer to the camouflaged moon,
    sea-mist drifting in?
I can't find you by day –
beach eager with surfers, loungers,
kids sculpting fragile castles grain by grain
                                 by grain.

Once, I believed in fairy tales, in things that lasted.
But each day waits with sudden mysteries,
offerings,
like dreams half-remembered
                from the night.

Refuge

lines from Maya Khosla

By evening the women are mountains
wrapped in dark shawls,
and the mountains are immoveable.
Hoarding bits of sun from the day,
their laps warm nests folded in fields.
They hum with voices of dragonflies, larkspur
delirious in psalms of shimmer and perfume:
a shelter for the sacred in each of us.

Of Roots

Light lingers
on this leaf,
that patch of grass,
cardinal insisting
from inside
the honeysuckle bush.
This is the moment
to be still.
Allow the sound
of chimes and crows
to lick your skin,
sink in
where your blood
rivers to your heart.
Is this the joy,
the peace we have
when we lean
into the sun?
See the echo of moon,
the blue above
eclipsing the stars
that sing
whether we see them
or not?
Bees nuzzle
clover, ants tracing
peonies, sweetness
tugged underground.
And now the grumble
of motors, of brakes
coughs through,
a siren screeching past.
Even so, the pines rise,
maples sugaring
both bud and root.
The most important labor
taking place
somewhere
out of sight.

Flesh Against Flesh

Blinded by sirens, reds and blues
lacerating the night,
a man hauls his daughter
out of the wide and grasping ditch,
car upside down on the street –
glass shattered, glittering the asphalt.

I want to turn away, to leave,
but traffic has stopped – nowhere to go
or turn around, and I remember
our last night together, memorizing
your face as we made love. You held me
until my tears dried, my cheek
on your chest, your hand through my hair.

Curled on the roadside, the man clutches
his girl, her arms embracing the stars.
I can't see her face, her ponytail dragging
the grass, but I see his – terror
                            comprehending the dark.

At the Joyce Kilmer National Forest

The forest, like a womb, pulses –
leaves waving in a canopy of tulip-poplars.
A forgotten trail opens ahead,
loosestrife and ferns almost obscuring
the earth, the roots of each quiet giant
ascending into blue. Ivy labors
across corded stumps, milky sap seeping
from the vines. Far below, Little Santeetlah Creek
rushes the rocks, a melody only sighing
up here where moss drapes stone and fallen trunks,
even beginning to skirt the barks,
where woodpeckers beat toward the hearts.
A vireo whistles from someplace
in the shadowy green, sunlight dappling
painted trillium and partridge-berry,
oak and sycamore guardians of this grove
stretching, still.

The Smell of Summer Grass

Oh, Gemini June,
    we thank you for greening branches
        and rain that rivers the fields, the forests
    where tadpoles wriggle and slide.

This month of long, longer days that curl
    into lingering, lasting nights
        where fireflies shine like cats' eyes
    and dog days weight the air.

We praise the cardinals' *chip, chip* in twilit cedars,
    the chickadees and wrens that wake us
        with ribbons of psalms. These we offer back –
    turquoise rectangles, teal ovals

where we splash and laugh;
    shade-swinging on porches, in hammocks;
        snails trailing morning dew
    before nestling under hydrangeas' pink and purple

singing time into slow-motion:
    to shape fairy gardens and wood forts,
        to churn ice cream for picnics, sweet
    peach juice dripping off our tongues.

I praise the sprinkler that wakes me after dawn,
    gardenias' vanilla incense cascading the lawn
        where cobwebs sulk in shadows,
    a dozen grills sparking backyard feasts.

An eight-year-old gifting neighbors with tomatoes
                                    she grew herself.

The Shape of Thorns

after *The Roses of Heliogabalus* by Sir Lawrence Alma-Tadema

An orgy of roses caress our flesh –
pink blossoms, pink tongues, pink skin entwine:
　　the gods look on, feast and feasting before them.
They leer as we yearn and shudder
　　under cascading petals, perfume drifting
like incense to the high table where they toast
　　our bemusement. No pricking thorns,
just silky smoothness that reminds us
　　of innocence, of desire, of acquiescence –
the Cailleach in flower form,
　　flute piping us to decadence, to destruction.

Midsummer Spell

Deluge overwhelms, divides the river
   in desperate rush and roil,
dryads clinging to mossy stones.
   Rhododendrons drip, petals sloughing,
drowning in muddy puddles along the path.
   Sheer madness to come out
when even the cuckoo hides quiet
   in the hedgerows. But the pull of this place
draws us further into the glen,
   off the trail where the woods close
around us. A greening of the air –
   the sudden silence a sign.
A twig cracks, smell of wet wood and loam
   rushing toward us, time tumbling around itself,
grasping to make sense of day, of cricket sighs, of us.
   Slipping in the in-between – moon and sun,
water and fire together before, behind us –
   breathing with us as the mountain shivers,
tugging us toward the white door.

Orion Holds Our Fate

Sun in Gemini, moon in Capricorn,
   mountains collide with wind
that rushes over the prairies
   and stutters across the seas.
Learning to live together is like flame
   kissing wood, rain beading ferns.
Grackles startle the sky, dark clouds
   of wings dusting the dimming blue.
A fox watches from the treeline,
   barks as twilight cracks the horizon.
June, December. Two halves break
   a whole, make a hole where the mystery
of *one* was kept. Triangulum
   may long to spiral Polaris,
but cold and hot do not often mix.
   We should have known we were luckless
from the start: your earth, my air.
   Like a stag and a wren
becoming friends. (Impossible.)

What I Owe the Fading Day

The rockface of mountains dreaming —Robert Hass

A tangle of pine waves from the rockface,
other leaves still lost, moldering in crevices
as winter abandons us. A skink hurtles
into a hollow, tugging a beetle's carapace
while a white sky crushes the horizon, spoils
the view with its blank weight.
Dreaming, the mountain, tinted with glacier lilies
and flowering currants, cools as twilight turns
gray, sighs into moonlight.

Night Song

I believe that you are hurting,
    I believe you have a song.
With a sky surging into redbuds,
    whispered spring steals winter's frost.

Though morning's lost her color
    to another hour of dusk,
the evening light still lingers,
    and you savor twilight's plunge.

If birthday candles weep
    another year now gone,
I believe the love you seeded
    is budding in the dark.

The feather falls out gently
    so another one can form,
the honey hive is sweetest
    wherever there's a swarm.

I believe the artist's painting
    of a cloudy, stormy sky,
and I believe she sees its wonder
    in the echo of her eye.

Though the cat has caught its bird
    and leaves whirl down in fall,
I believe that root and wing
    are strongest after all.

As Light Dissolves

Clouds, dappling leaf and sky, drift orange
then yellow before disappearing altogether,
blankets of lightning bugs blinking the dusk.
Time for horses to return to their stalls,
to make peace of disputes,
crickets and frogs singing to the stars.
Barley Moon ignites the edges of ebony clouds,
salmon spawning in the riverbeds
past hazelwood thickets and clusters of holly.
The heat of summer lingers, but evening traces
the veins, grazes the tips of leaves
now past the slipping light.

The Surface of Water

The surface of water holds our shame,
ripples and wraps it close,
drowns all sorrow and joy, extinguishes their flame.

We watch as it sinks and try to reclaim
some of the good that we chose,
but the surface of water holds our shame.

Even as children just learning to name,
we put on our masks, never exposed,
drowned all sorrow and joy, extinguished their flame.

And as we grew and hoarded we became
collectors of stone and baggage imposed.
But the surface of water holds our shame,

lets it puddle and pool in a circular frame.
Then the current laps over, diffuses its blow,
drowns all sorrow and joy, extinguishes their flame.

And the sun and the moon reflect just the same,
winter's frosty hue and summer's sweet rose.
The surface of water holds our shame,
drowns all sorrow and joy, extinguishes their flame.

Winter, Taking Root

A fugitive blue sneaks through
    the robe of dusk, mauve and purple
trembling in mist. Magnolias spy
    with cardinal eyes, and I eavesdrop
as stars hum a sickle moon into the sky.
    Abelia perfumes the air
and shadows calico the yard:
    Wait! Wait!
The edge of summer, the lip of change
    kisses this hour,
and we're all bewitched by whispering
    stones and starshine.

Interpreting the Night

Moth moon sings, calls the sleepers
    into labyrinths where sirens whirl
and tumble, fluting blue tunes
    that drift deep, deeper across the coral, the rock.
Filaments of salt crack, tickle
    the shore, sand slipping
like the desert shifts its hills and valleys.
    Wind circles into siroccos that lift dreamers
over the aches, the wounds of days
    cowering in lonely spaces.
A dragonfly zips through haze, through synapses,
    tugs tendrils of dreams still echoing
as sunlight swells the room.

IV.

Where is the heart

Dr Tarr's Trout Farm

    Laurel Bloomery, Tennessee

Near Backbone Rock, somewhere
   between Mountain City and Damascus,
the faded sign droops
   beside a pockmarked road,
wild roses rambling the open gate.

Seven ponds span the glade,
   cress and red clover crowding the edges
in twisted thickets, a rabbit skittering
   into the undergrowth. A natural spring spills
into the first two, but clay pipes
   fractured along the way, shards
tumbled to the side. No trout now
   in these algae-painted pools.
Still, still waters.

Memories of laughter tangle
   the woodoats, curve around gnarled trunks
where ghost-children shadow black gum and hickory,
   dangle bait from reels and poles,
grandfathers' lessons haunting the leaves.

Sun slanting low unveils the dragonflies,
   the gnats skipping and dimpling the water.
Lone frog *chukk, chukk*ing nearby,
   an owl, a mourning dove compete
for the most sorrow.

Where is the heart of the trout?
   In the hidden wellspring, in the crow
     feasting near the roots.
Where is the heart of the man?
   In the rock ranged around this farm, these ponds.
     Still guarding, guiding, protecting:
a phantom wind blowing in.

The Song Gathers

Monarchs frisk the thistle,
stash nectar and pearls of pollen,
desire oozing legs and bellies.
Shadows feather the field,
singing September's
fading blue. The woods throb
with heat,   more heat –

nothing whispering
in the underbrush except dust,
which scatters to a sickle moon
slicing the noon sky.
Lethargy seeps into skin, blood
like swimming in a clouded lake,
air steamed with haze – eyes closing

with memory   and dream.

Daughters of the Wind

When you gave me the seeds
   to the kingdom of seas, I didn't know
the ocean would unfold

in plumes and drops, bits of blue
   snagging, scabbing rock and sand,
the coast itself a ceaseless puzzle.

I sowed them in September's charm,
   serenaded the bride while a wild swan dreamed
in a whirlwind – petals and tentacles

   reaching, reaching.

Every day in woods or sea, anemones
   beckon me, sting my mind, beauty
with no sweetness to spare.

Salt tanging my tongue,
   sun swimming through clouds.
Rain painting my face.

Beauty Enough

Mud pools in the back yard,
grass defeated – soggy and stooped.
A squirrel whiskers the limb
of an oak, flings itself into the gray void.
Katydids stereo the coming dark,
applaud the rising moon.

Valkyrie

Back when the earth ran red, fire
   and blood steaming the streets, the fields,
      when wings were in fashion,
     and we soared to each occasion –
as tiny as dandelion seeds, as large as eagles.
When women were birds, we were carrion-
   feeders, claws seizing the night.
     No nightingale songs for us.
       We wheeled over battles, picked the victor,
         the victim – didn't matter to Odin
     whether their souls rested or rotted.
   But it mattered to us.
We could decide by smile, by muscle.
   Even by family.
     Sometimes death was too good.
       A more punishing path charted for them
         where sulfur and smoke scorches forever.
     Spears pierced bodies, shields shattered,
impotent swords slumped from hands
   now open, like their eyes, to the sky.
     A sky they never noticed before
    full of circling shadows, our mercy no more
than a beak tearing flesh, the sound
      of wings lifting and fading away.

Moonwitching

Dry bones rattling, rattling.
   Cobweb-covered, dust-smothered,

they rise, they rise.

   Full moon, blue moon –
werewolf soon?

   A shiver, a shake, whispers
in the shadows as they multiply.

   Stars in free-fall, no more recall
when Pegasus flies.

   Jack o'lantern grinning,
leaves swirling and spinning
   in a wind tinged with frost.

What's the price? What's the cost
   on a dark and stormy night
while the ravens in flight,
   and their purple-black sheen
shimmers in the light?

   Haystacks scratch a charcoal sky,
clouds scumble and spit fangs of ice.

   Dry bones rattling, battling,
gravestones shattering: rise.
   Rise.

Evensong

On my porch I watch the storm come in –
   see it sweep across the yard and then
each drop tumbles from the eaves.

Flapping from porch to tree, a house finch
   chitters at me. Nest in my door-wreath again,
she bounces from branch to twig,
   eyes me then flusters in to feed her chicks.

I am here, with her, with them.

Beyond the clouds stars gather,
   the darkness between them nothing.
Still they blink, they glow
   though whispering mist consumes them.

Wind kicks spray onto the porch, my feet,
   and I laugh. Night slips in. The finch tucks
her wings, settles into straw and down,

clear notes piping into the sky.

The Promise of Stars

A confetti of frost scatters
   the town square, chambers of white
stitched with shadow and ice.

It's raining stars and an owl whirrs,
   a fox hounding the constellations.

Hope pressed to our chests, we sleep.
   Clouds erase the slipper moon,
the rubble, the tin-tacked barns.

Shades of night deepen – mercy perching
   in bare branches like polished silver.

All Shall Be Well

Loosestrife waves from the woods,
dew-damp petals luminous,

a beacon in shadows babbling
by the stream. No news from the world –

good news. Here, with no connection
beyond this cabin, these trails,

my mind centers on the pulse
and churn of water below.

Pink-tipped rhododendron creates clouds
around the cove bound by ridge and mountain,

creek and stone. A green womb that holds
back the sun, collects pockets of rock and foam.

Time has no meaning – only a partial sky
that brightens and dims, rim of moon calling

me to join the whippoorwills, an owl –
a few stars to remind me I'm not alone.

Hymn

Take off your shoes –

midnight's thirst slaked by cup, by storm
   your arm on pillows, waits to embrace me
sunrise washes the horizon pink and gold
   sheets flap in summer breezes, wrapping us at night
wrens scuffle the porch rail, chorus enough
   coffee infuses the air with morning
lake echoes tree, cloud – a double portion of joy
   a pocketful of mints, one for each grandchild
raindrops pearl the oak leaves
   woodpecker drums a hollow tree
a cat purrs on your lap, kneads you in sleep
   scarlet maples flame the sky
children's voices on the school bus sing through the air
   the neighbor's dog waits to play, snuffles for treats
snowflakes stray from woolly clouds
   melodies half-remembered, hummed in a shower
twilight sparks with fireflies, stars
   your heartbeat under my cheek

    – for this is holy ground

A Song Already There

You follow steppingstones
　　to open fields. A startle of blackbirds surges,
dark wings wheeling around you –
　　　everything in you rising with them.

At autumn's threshold even the robin sings
　　through the sycamores' sighs,
and white-foam laughs across the sea,
　　　summer preserved in the deep blue
　　though frost sketches the high tide line.

Only stone or glass hearts break.
　　The rest of us muscle through each day
savoring the rainbow after the rage,
　　　the honey after the sting –

　　the ocean whispering the shore again,
just where you kneel.

About the Author

KB Ballentine resides in Chattanooga, Tennessee, and teaches composition, creative writing, theatre arts, and literature to high school and college students in addition to conducting writing workshops throughout the United States.

Ballentine received her MFA in Creative Writing, Poetry, from Lesley University, Cambridge, MA.

Ballentine's seventh collection *Edge of the Echo* was published with Iris Press in 2021. Other collections of poetry are *The Light Tears Loose* (Blue Light Press 2019), *Almost Everything, Almost Nothing* (Middle Creek Publishing 2017), the 2016 Blue Light Press Book Award winner *The Perfume of Leaving* was preceded by *What Comes of Waiting* (2013), also by Blue Light Press. *Fragments of Light* (2009) and *Gathering Stones* (2008) were published by Celtic Cat Publishing.

Published in numerous literary journals and anthologies, Ballentine was awarded the Libba Moore Gray Poetry Prize in 2016, in 2014 she was a finalist for the Ron Rash Poetry Award, an Opera Omaha finalist in 2008, a 2007 finalist for the Ruth Stone Prize in Poetry, and in 2006 a finalist for the Joy Harjo Poetry Award. She was a recipient of the Dorothy Sargent Rosenberg Poetry Prize in 2006 and in 2007.

Learn more about KB Ballentine at www.kbballentine.com.

www.ingramcontent.com/pod-product-compliance
Lightning Source LLC
Chambersburg PA
CBHW031158160426
43193CB00008B/430